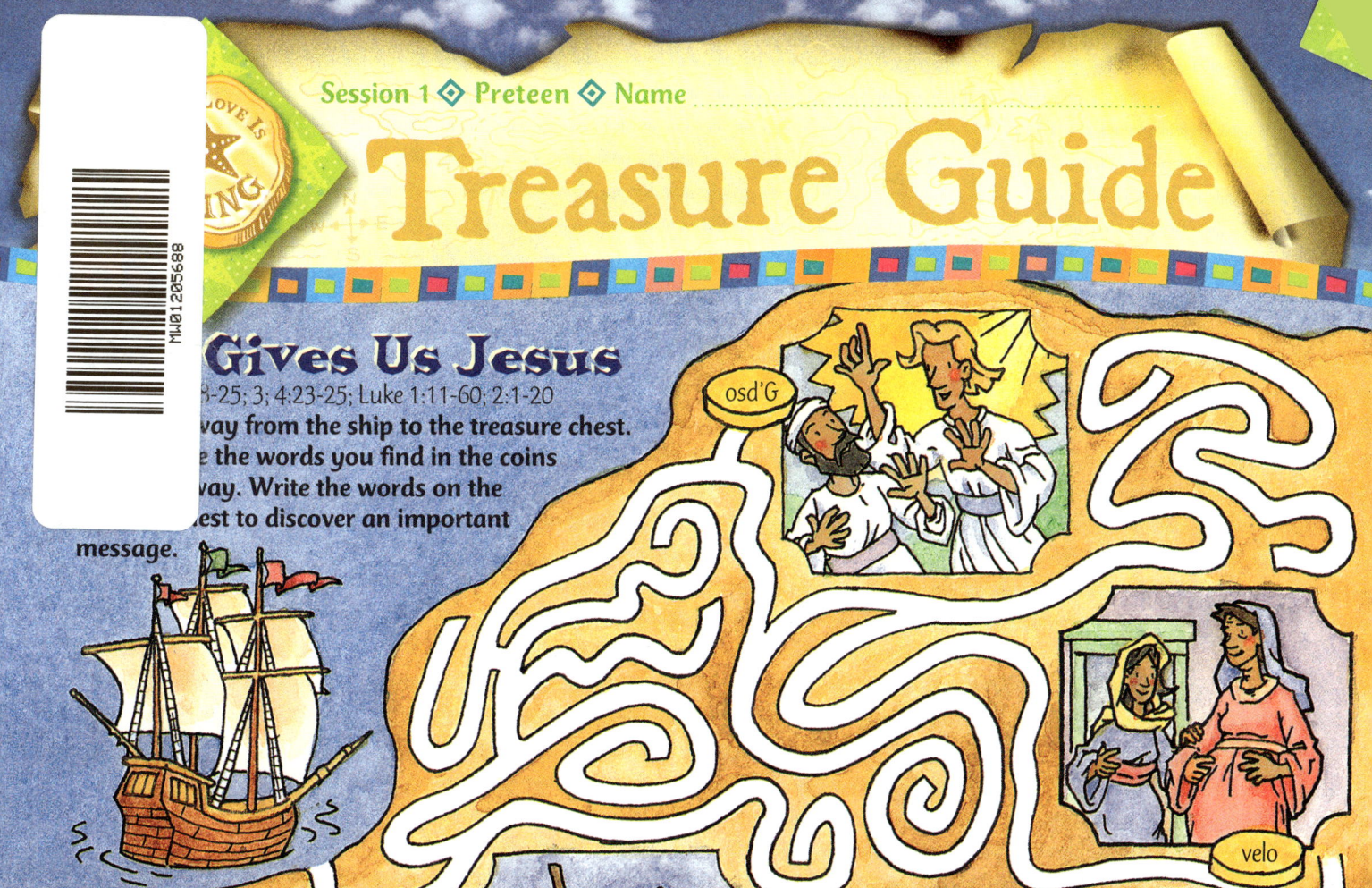

Love-ly Choices

For each situation below, write two good ways the kid in the picture could show God's love.

Bible Memory Verse

"This is how God showed his love among us: He sent his one and only Son into the world that we might live through him."
1 John 4:9

Here's the situation:

Kyle is the worst batter on the team. His teammates tease him and point out everything he does wrong. Sam knows this upsets Kyle, but

Sam could...

Or he could...

Session 2 ◇ Preteen ◇ Name ....

Treasure Guide

God's Love Is KIND

Jesus Helps a Young Girl and a Sick Woman

Matthew 9:18-26; Mark 5:21-43; Luke 8:40-56

Fill in the blanks to complete each story caption. Then draw a line starting at the boat to connect each island in story order.

Jesus helped people and _____ them about God's love.

Jesus stopped to _____ the woman because of her _____.

Session 3 ◆ Preteen ◆ Name ....

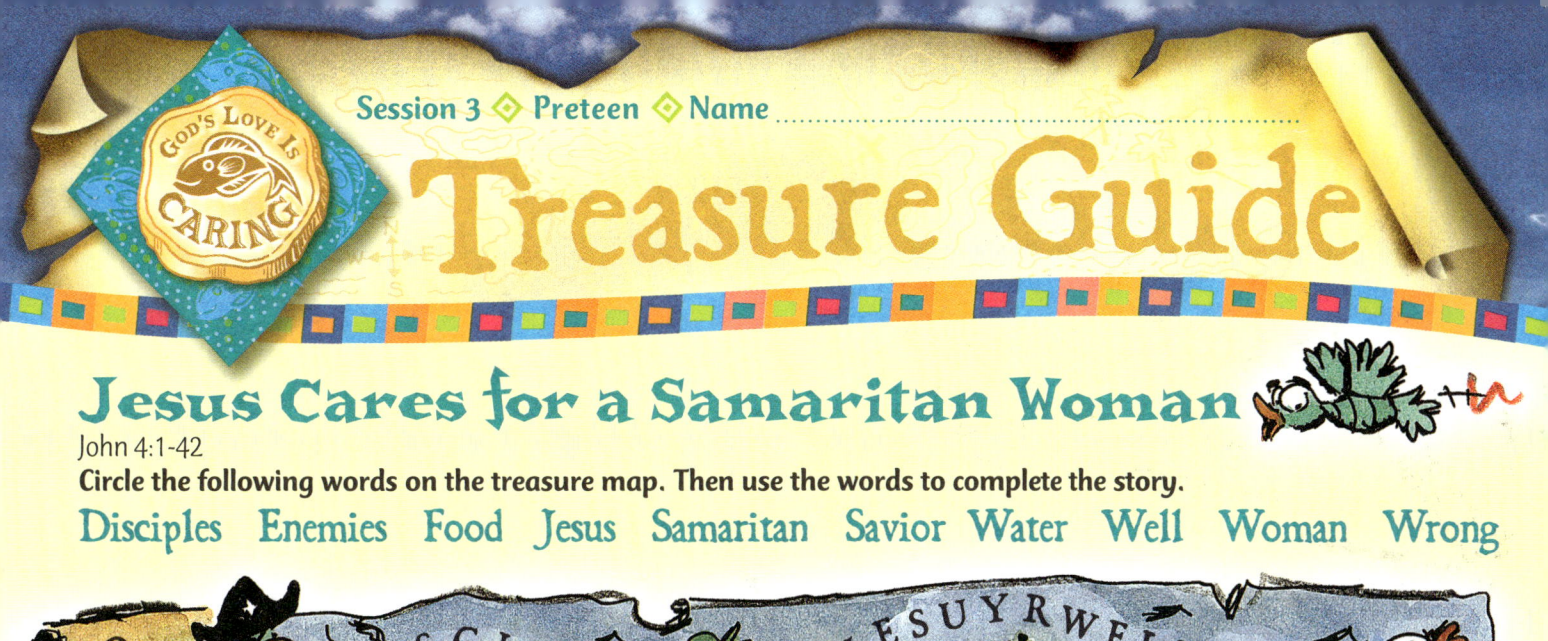

God's Love Is CARING

Treasure Guide

Jesus Cares for a Samaritan Woman
John 4:1-42

Circle the following words on the treasure map. Then use the words to complete the story.

Disciples   Enemies   Food   Jesus   Samaritan   Savior   Water   Well   Woman   Wrong

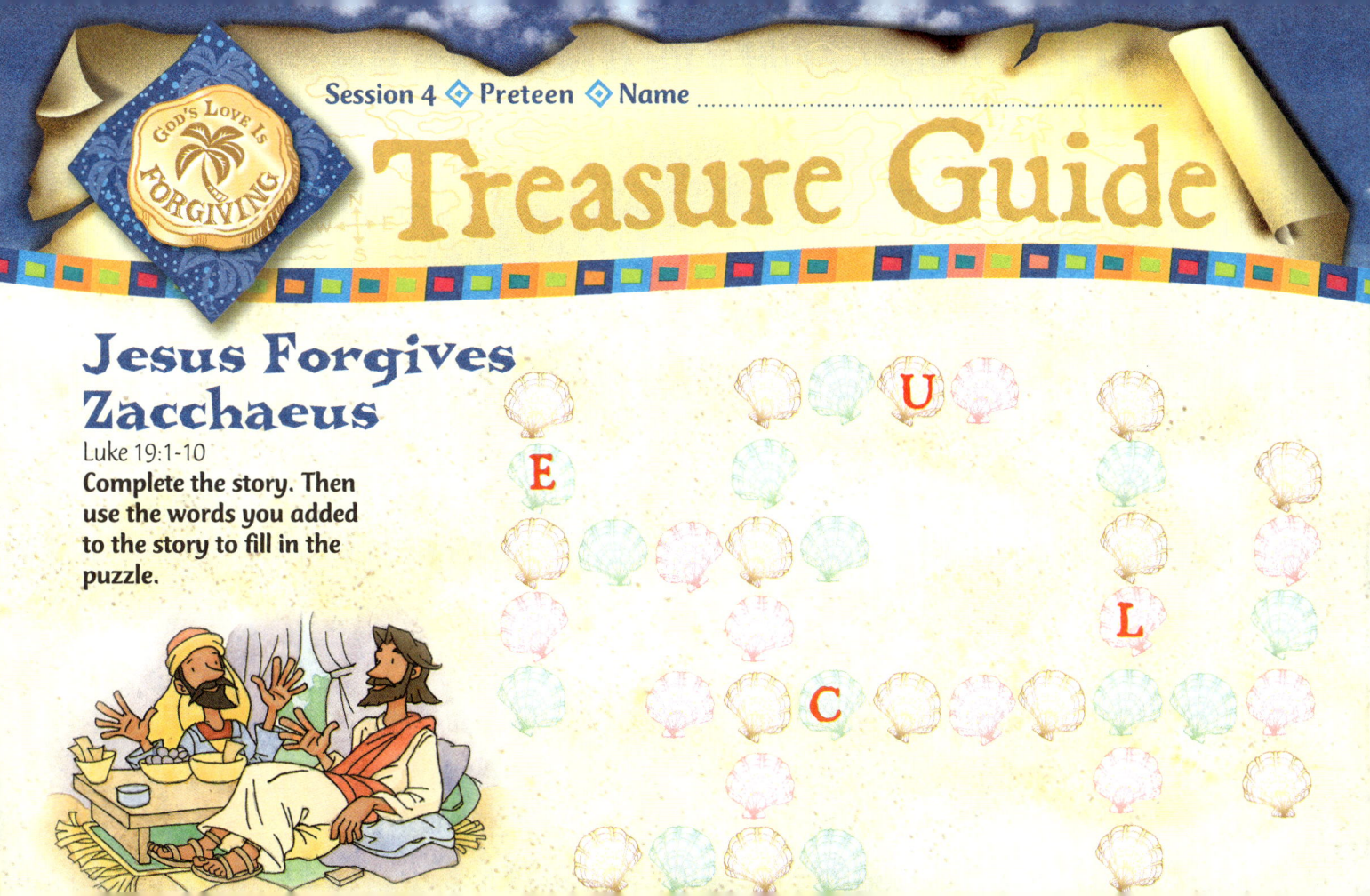

Parrot Problems

Pete's pal Penelope asked permission to take Pete's pet parrot, Polly, to the pool party. Pete said no, but Penelope did it anyway. Polly flew away! **Complete the chart below to show how Pete and Penelope can show God's love.**

Bible Memory Verse

"[Love] is not easily angered, it keeps no record of wrongs. Love does not delight in evil but rejoices with the truth."
1 Corinthians 13:5-6

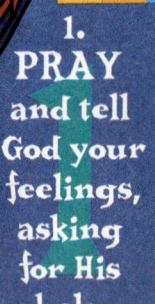

1. **PRAY** and tell God your feelings, asking for His help.

2.

How can Penelope make amends with Pete?

Dear God,

I feel _____
_____.

Please help me to _____
_____.

How might Pete feel?

How can Pete forgive Penelope?

Dear God,

I feel _____
_____.

Please help me to _____
_____.

How might Penelope feel?

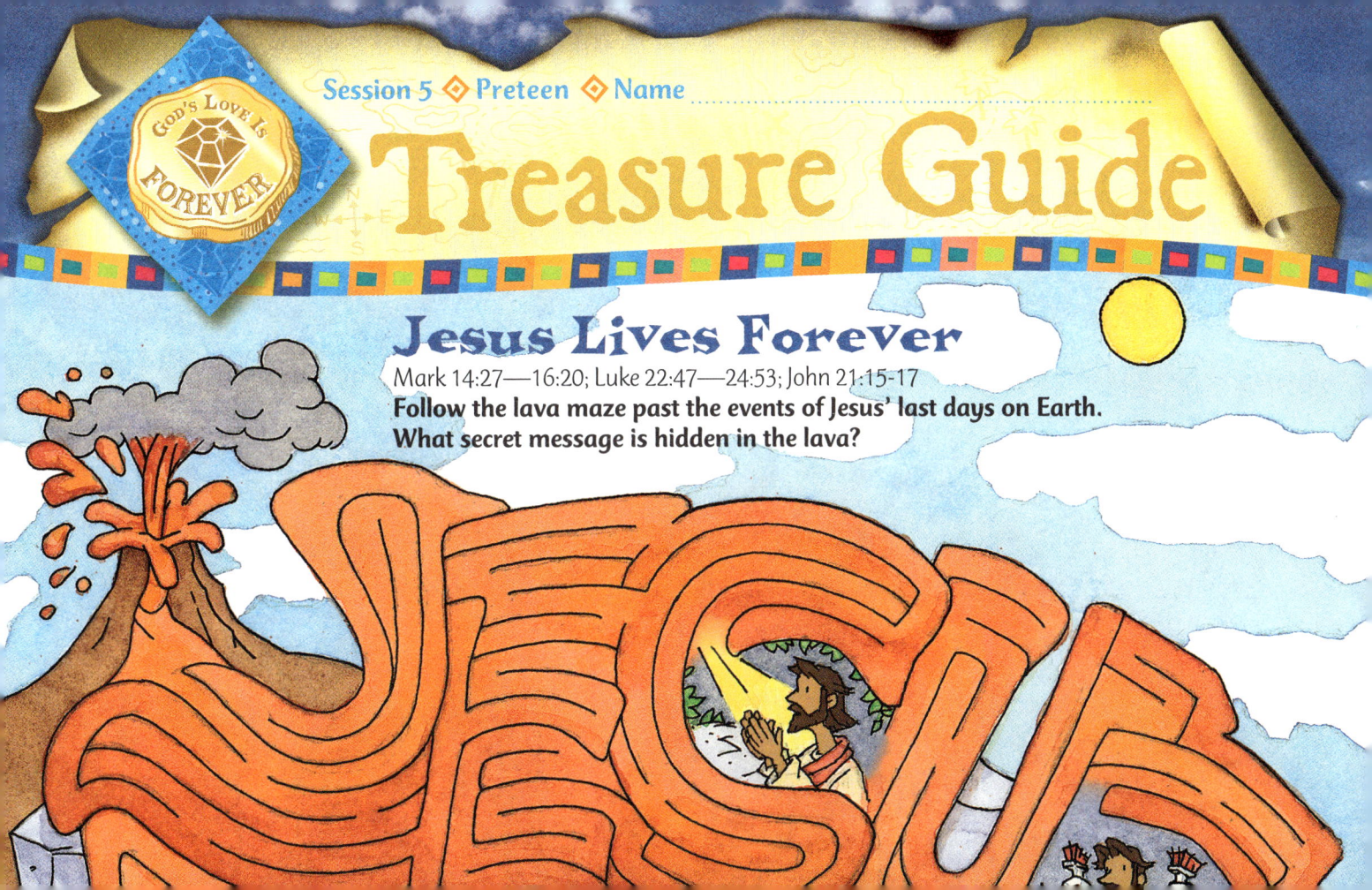

Dora's Dreadfulest Day

Dora's last day on SonTreasure Island was downright dreadful. Anything that COULD go wrong DID go wrong! Below each photo, tell how remembering God's love would make a difference in what Dora does AFTER each event.

Bible Memory Verse

"[Love] always protects, always trusts, always hopes, always perseveres. Love never fails."
1 Corinthians 13:7-8

Hailey bumped Dora, causing Dora to drop her camera into the sea!

At lunch, Dora discovered that she's allergic to lobster!

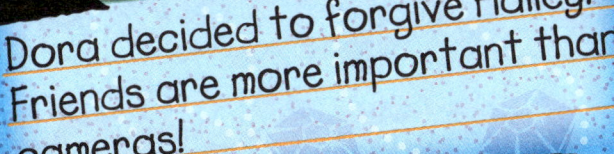
Dora decided to forgive Hailey. Friends are more important than cameras!

On the way to the airport, Dora lost her patience and said something mean to Hailey.

When she got home, Dora found out that her luggage had been sent to Kathmandu instead of Kansas!

© Gospel Light. **It is illegal to photocopy or reproduce this material in any form.**

2. about how the other person may feel.

☐ Happy ☐ Sad ☐ Angry
☐ _____ ☐ Dizzy ☐ Worried

☐ Afraid ☐ Happy ☐ Bored
☐ _____ ☐ Embarrassed ☐ Sad

---

3. TALK with the person honestly about the problem.

What could Penelope say?
☐ I'm sorry if you were offended.
☐ I'm sorry. I should have listened to you.
☐ I'm sure you can find another bird.
☐ _____

What could Pete say?
☐ I never want to talk to you again!
☐ I know you didn't mean to lose Polly.
☐ I really miss Polly.
☐ _____

---

4. CHOOSE to treat the person with love.

Draw something Penelope could do to make amends for losing Polly.

Draw something Pete could do to show that he forgives Penelope.

© Gospel Light. **It is illegal to photocopy or reproduce this material in any form.**

Whenever __ __ __ __ __ __ __ __ came to __ __ __ __ __ __ __ people's taxes, he cheated them and took more money than they owed! One day he heard that __ __ __ __ __ was visiting his town. Because Zacchaeus was too short to see over the crowd, he climbed a __ __ __ __ to get a better look. When Jesus saw him, He said, "Zacchaeus, come down! I want to visit your __ __ __ __ __." Zacchaeus was honored that Jesus would talk to him! Because Jesus showed God's love, Zacchaeus felt __ __ __ __ __ for the wrong things he had done. He promised to give half of his money to the poor and to pay back everyone that he had cheated __ __ __ __ times the amount! Jesus __ __ __ __ __ __ __ Zacchaeus, and He will do the same for us, when we are sorry.

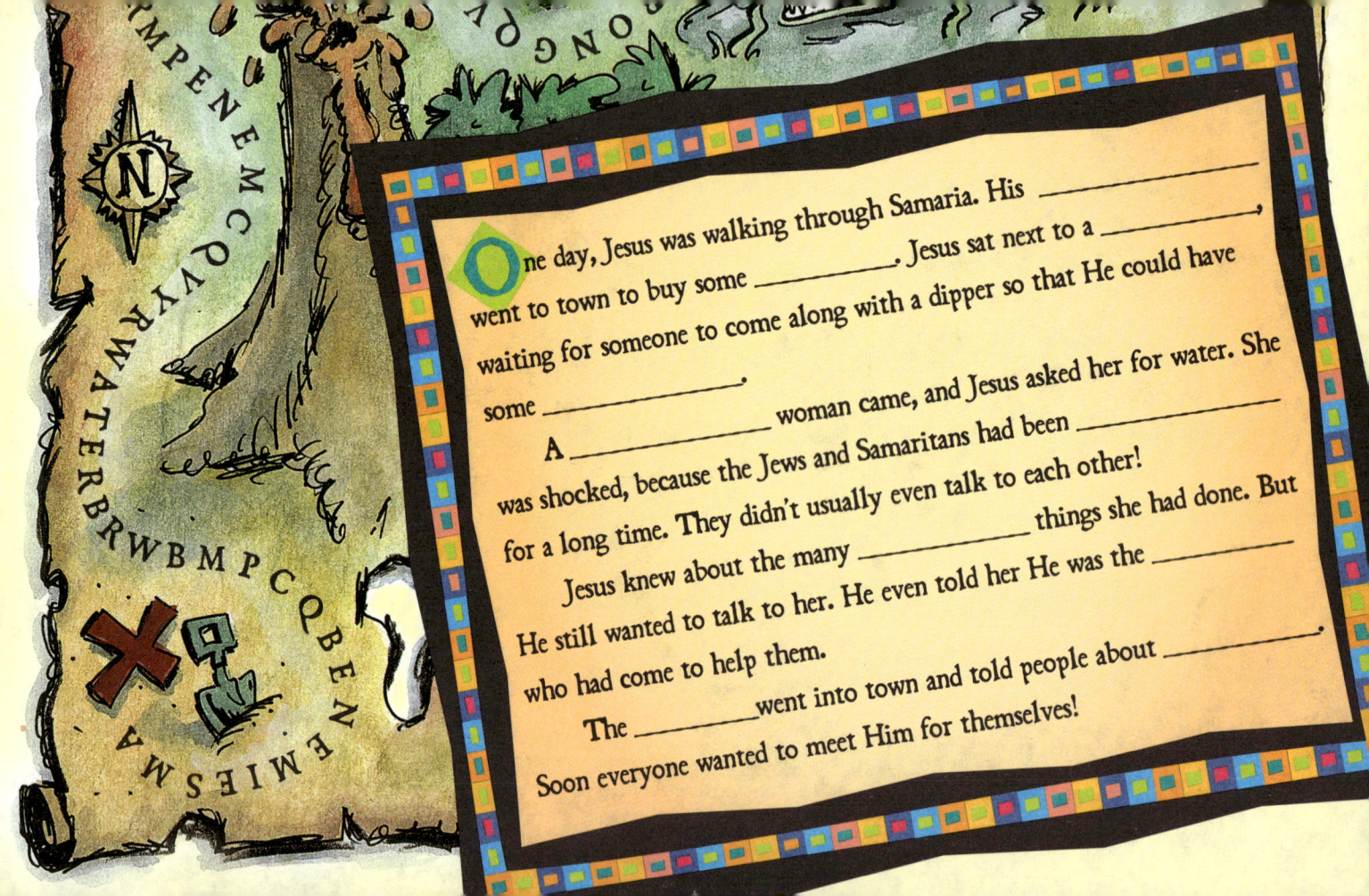

One day, Jesus was walking through Samaria. His _____ went to town to buy some _____. Jesus sat next to a _____, waiting for someone to come along with a dipper so that He could have some _____.

A _____ woman came, and Jesus asked her for water. She was shocked, because the Jews and Samaritans had been _____ for a long time. They didn't usually even talk to each other! Jesus knew about the many _____ things she had done. But He still wanted to talk to her. He even told her He was the _____ who had come to help them.

The _____ went into town and told people about _____. Soon everyone wanted to meet Him for themselves!

Here's the situation:

Sarah's little sister copies everything she does. She dresses like her, talks like her and has the same beach bag. Now she's started copying Sarah's hairstyle!

Sarah could...

Or she could...

© Gospel Light.
It is illegal to photocopy or reproduce this material in any form.